W9-AUI-783

WITHDRAWN

Let's Celebrate
American Holidays

Columbus Day

Aaron Carr

LA GRANGE PUBLIC LIBRARY
10 W. COSSITT AVE.
LA GRANGE, IL 60525
708.215.3200

COLUMBUS CITIZENS FOUNDATION

LET'S READ
AV2 BY WEIGL™
ADDED VALUE • AUDIO VISUAL

www.av2books.com

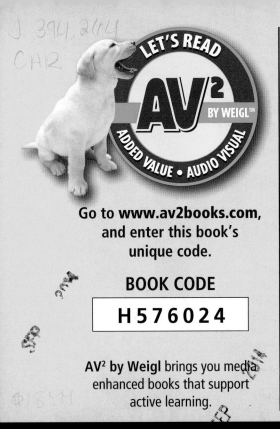

LET'S READ

AV²

BY WEIGL™

ADDED VALUE • AUDIO VISUAL

Go to **www.av2books.com**, and enter this book's unique code.

BOOK CODE

H576024

AV² by Weigl brings you media enhanced books that support active learning.

AV² provides enriched content that supplements and complements this book. Weigl's AV² books strive to create inspired learning and engage young minds in a total learning experience.

Your AV² Media Enhanced books come alive with...

Audio
Listen to sections of the book read aloud.

Video
Watch informative video clips.

Embedded Weblinks
Gain additional information for research.

Try This!
Complete activities and hands-on experiments.

Key Words
Study vocabulary, and complete a matching word activity.

Quizzes
Test your knowledge.

Slide Show
View images and captions, and prepare a presentation.

... and much, much more!

Published by AV² by Weigl
350 5th Avenue, 59th Floor New York, NY 10118
Websites: www.av2books.com www.weigl.com

Library of Congress Control Number: 2014934874

ISBN 978-1-4896-1122-2 (hardcover)
ISBN 978-1-4896-1123-9 (softcover)
ISBN 978-1-4896-1124-6 (single user eBook)
ISBN 978-1-4896-1125-3 (multi-user eBook)

Printed in the United States of America in North Mankato, Minnesota
1 2 3 4 5 6 7 8 9 0 18 17 16 15 14

052014
WEP150314

Project Coordinator: Katie Gillespie   Design and Layout: Ana Maria Vidal

Weigl acknowledges Getty Images as the primary image supplier for this title.

2

Let's Celebrate American Holidays
Columbus Day

CONTENTS

Log on to www.av2books.com

Columbus Day is celebrated on the second Monday in October. It is a day to remember an Italian explorer named Christopher Columbus and his 1492 trip to the Americas.

Columbus was the first European explorer to arrive in the Americas after the Vikings.

Columbus was trying to find a route from Europe to Asia. He thought he could get to Asia in a few days by sailing west.

Columbus had three ships called the *Nina*, the *Pinta*, and the *Santa Maria*.

Italian Americans wanted to honor Columbus for his great journey. They held the first celebration in 1792 in New York City.

Columbus Day was first made a national holiday by President Benjamin Harrison in 1892.

The president wanted a holiday to celebrate all Americans. Columbus Day was meant to honor the American Indians and the many Italians who later came to America.

Today, Columbus Day events take place across the United States. Most celebrations are held in Italian-American communities.

The largest Columbus Day events take place in New York and San Francisco.

On Columbus Day, people celebrate Italian American culture. They eat Italian foods such as pasta and crusty bread.

People gather on Columbus Day to see large parades. The parades may have dancing, music, and people waving Italian flags.

Almost one million people come to watch the Columbus Day Parade in New York City each year.

17

Some people like to spend time with friends and family on Columbus Day. There are special outdoor activities such as boat races.

On Columbus Day, sailors race their boats off the coast of Florida.

Columbus Day is a time to fly the Italian flag. This is a way for Italian Americans to show pride in their heritage.

COLUMBUS DAY FACTS

These pages provide more detail about the interesting facts found in the book. They are intended to be used by adults as a learning support to help young readers round out their knowledge of each holiday featured in the *Let's Celebrate American Holidays* series.

Pages 4–5

Columbus Day is celebrated on the second Monday in October. On October 12, 1492, Italian explorer Christopher Columbus arrived in what would later be known as the Americas. This was the first time a European explorer landed here since the Vikings sailed to North America 500 years earlier. Columbus's arrival marked the beginning of a period of exploration and settlement of the New World.

Pages 6–7

Columbus was trying to find a route from Europe to Asia. European nations wanted to establish a trade route by sea with Asia to replace the overland Silk Road. Kings and queens funded explorers to search for this route. Most searched the coast of Africa, looking for an eastern route. Columbus, however, believed a western route across the Atlantic would be faster.

Pages 8–9

Italian Americans wanted to honor Columbus for his great journey. In 1792, a group of Italian Americans in New York City decided to celebrate Columbus's achievement with a parade. This was the 300th anniversary of his landing in the New World. President Benjamin Harrison proclaimed Columbus Day to be a national holiday 100 years later.

Pages 10–11

The president wanted a holiday to celebrate all Americans. In 1892, Columbus Day became the first holiday in the United States to honor both the immigrants who flocked to the United States in great numbers and the American Indians who were already there when Columbus arrived. It was a special day to celebrate the land and all of its people.

Today, Columbus Day events take place across the United States. Most celebrations are held in Italian-American communities.

The largest Columbus Day events take place in New York and San Francisco.

Today, Columbus Day events take place across the United States. The largest Columbus Day celebrations take place in New York City. Other large parades and festivals are held in cities across the country, such as Chicago and San Francisco. The majority of the festivities are held by people of Italian American heritage.

On Columbus Day, people celebrate Italian American culture. They eat Italian foods such as pasta and crusty bread.

On Columbus Day, people celebrate Italian American culture. Columbus Day is an occasion for Italian Americans to celebrate the achievements of fellow Italian, Christopher Columbus. Italian foods, music, and dance are often staples of Columbus Day celebrations.

People gather on Columbus Day to see large parades. The parades may have dancing, music, and people waving Italian flags.

Almost one million people come to watch the Columbus Day Parade in New York City each year.

People gather on Columbus Day to see large parades. These parades feature floats, marching bands, dancers, and large numbers of people who just want to march in the parade. At the Annual Columbus Day Parade in New York City, 35,000 people gather to march, and there are nearly one million spectators. Some cities host a full weekend of events, including dancing, music, and festivals.

Some people like to spend time with friends and family on Columbus Day. There are special outdoor activities such as boat races.

On Columbus Day, sailors race their boats off the coast of Florida.

Some people like to spend time with friends and family on Columbus Day. Many people get out and enjoy Columbus Day festivities, while others use this holiday as an opportunity to spend time with their friends and family. In Miami, Florida, people take a different approach to the holiday. There, sailors have been taking part in an annual Columbus Day regatta, or boat race, since 1954.

Columbus Day is a time to fly the Italian flag. This is a way for Italian Americans to show pride in their heritage.

Columbus Day is a time to fly the Italian flag. In order to celebrate their Italian American heritage, many people carry flags, drape them over themselves, and fly them from buildings on Columbus Day. People also dress in the green, white, and red colors of the flag or paint these colors on their faces or bodies.

KEY WORDS

Research has shown that as much as 65 percent of all written material published in English is made up of 300 words. These 300 words cannot be taught using pictures or learned by sounding them out. They must be recognized by sight. This book contains 68 common sight words to help young readers improve their reading fluency and comprehension. This book also teaches young readers several important content words, such as proper nouns. These words are paired with pictures to aid in learning and improve understanding.

Page	Sight Words First Appearance
4	a, after, an, and, day, first, his, in, is, it, named, on, second, the, to, was
7	by, could, few, find, from, get, had, he, thought, three
8	Americans, for, great, they
9	made
11	all, came, later, many, who
12	are, most, place, take
15	as, eat, foods, people, such
16	almost, come, each, have, large, may, one, see, watch, year
19	family, like, of, off, some, their, there, time, with
21	show, this, way, white

Page	Content Words First Appearance
4	Americas, Christopher Columbus, Columbus Day, explorer, Monday, October, trip, Vikings
7	Asia, Europe, Nina, Pinta, route, Santa Maria, ships, west
8	celebration, journey, New York City
9	holiday, President Benjamin Harrison
11	American Indians, Italians
12	communities, San Francisco, United States
15	bread, culture, pasta
16	Columbus Day Parade, dancing, flags, million, music,
18	activities, boats, coast, Florida, friends, sailors, races
21	colors, heritage, pride